A passion for prayer

STORMIE OMARTIAN

Paintings by

Simon Bull

HARVEST HOUSE PUBLISHERS

EUGENE, OREGON

A passion for prayer

Text Copyright © 2002 by Stormie Omartian
Published by Harvest House Publishers
Eugene, Oregon 97402

ISBN 0-7369-0893-5

Media Arts Group, Inc.
900 Lightpost Way
Morgan Hill, CA 95037
1.800.366.3733

Text from this book previously appeared in *The Power of a Praying® Wife*
(Harvest House Publishers, 1997), *The Power of a Praying® Parent* (Harvest House Publishers, 1995)
and *The Power of a Praying® Husband* (Harvest House Publishers, 2001).

Design & production by Koechel Peterson and Associates, Minneapolis, Minnesota

Printed in Hong Kong

02 03 04 05 06 07 08 09 10 11 / NG / 10 9 8 7 6 5 4 3 2 1

prayer

does not enable
us to do a greater
work for God.

prayer is

a greater work
for God.

—Thomas Chalmers

A PASSION *for* PRAYER

PRAYER IS MUCH MORE than just giving a list of desires to God, as if He were the great Sugar Daddy/Santa Claus in the sky. Prayer is acknowledging and experiencing the presence of God and inviting His presence into our lives and circumstances. It's seeking the presence of God and releasing the power of God which gives us the means to overcome any problem.

Prayer is the soul's sincere desire,
Uttered or unexpressed,
The motion of a hidden fire
That trembles in the breast.
JAMES MONTGOMERY

THE BIBLE SAYS, "Whatever you bind on earth will be bound in heaven, and whatever you loose on earth will be loosed in heaven" (Matthew 18:18). God gives us authority on earth. When we take that authority, God releases power to us from heaven. Because it's God's power and not ours, we become the vessel through which His power flows. When we pray, we bring that power to bear upon everything we are praying about, and we allow the power of God to work through our powerlessness. When we pray, we are humbling ourselves before God and saying, "I need Your presence and Your power, Lord. I can't do this without You." When we don't pray, it's like saying we have no need of anything outside of ourselves.

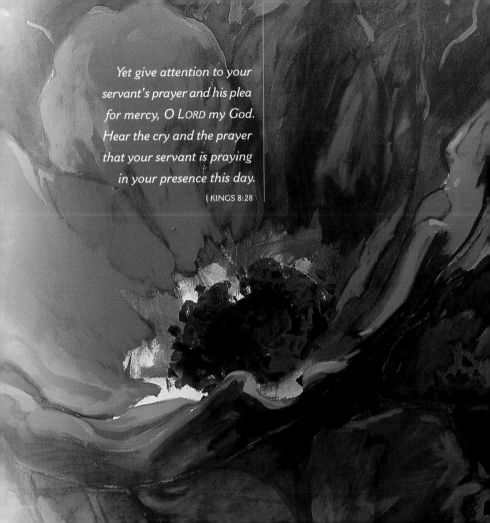

*Yet give attention to your
servant's prayer and his plea
for mercy, O LORD my God.
Hear the cry and the prayer
that your servant is praying
in your presence this day.*

1 KINGS 8:28

praying

PRAYING IN THE NAME OF JESUS is a major key to God's power. Jesus said, "Most assuredly, I say to you, whatever you ask the Father in My name He will give you" (John 16:23). Praying in the name of Jesus gives us authority over the enemy and proves we have faith in God to do what His Word promises. God knows our thoughts and our needs, but He responds to our prayers. That's because He always gives us a choice about everything, including whether we will trust Him and obey by praying in Jesus' name.

> *Of all duties, prayer certainly*
> *is the sweetest and most easy.*
> LAURENCE STERNE

Whatever you ask in My name, that I will do, that the Father may be glorified in the Son. If you ask anything in My name, I will do it.

JOHN 14:13-14

Do what you can do,
and pray for what you cannot do.
ST. AUGUSTINE

PRAYING NOT ONLY AFFECTS US, it also reaches out and touches those for whom we pray. We are asking God to make His presence a part of their lives and work powerfully in their behalf. That doesn't mean there will always be an immediate response. Sometimes it can take days, weeks, months, or even years. But our prayers are never lost or meaningless. If we are praying, something is happening, whether we can see it or not. The Bible says, "The effective, fervent prayer of a righteous man avails much" (James 5:16). All that needs to happen in our lives cannot happen without the presence and power of God. Prayer invites and ignites both.

The man who kneels to God
can stand up to anything.

LOUIS H. EVANS, JR.

Lord,

create in me a clean heart
and renew a right spirit within me.

show me

where my attitude
and thoughts are not what
you would have them to be.
convict me when I am
being unforgiving.

Help me

to let go of any anger, so that confusion will
not have a place in my mind. If there is
behavior in me that needs to change, enable
me to make changes that last.

whatever

you reveal to me,
I will confess to you as sin.
Enable me to be the person that
you created me to be.

I BELIEVE IN THE POWER of prayer. It's not enough to pray only for the concerns of the moment; we need to pray for the future, and we need to pray against the effects of past events. When King David was depressed over what had happened in his life and fearful about future consequences (Psalm 143), he didn't just say, "Oh, well, whatever will be, will be." He cried out to God about the past, present, and future of his life. He prayed about everything. And that is exactly what we must do as well.

Prayer is a powerful thing, for God has
bound and tied himself thereto.
None can believe how powerful prayer is,
and what it is able to effect,
but those who have learned it by experience.

MARTIN LUTHER

faithful

WHEN WE EMPLOY GOD'S WORD in prayer, we are laying hold of the promises He gives us. Through His Word, God guides us, speaks to us, and reminds us He is faithful. In that way, He builds faith in our hearts and enables us to understand His heart. This helps us to pray boldly in faith, knowing exactly what is His truth, His will, and our authority.

If I really wanted to pray I'll tell you what I'd do. I'd go out into a great big field all alone or into the deep, deep woods, and I'd look up into the sky- up- up- up- into that lovely blue sky that looks as if there was no end to its blueness. And then I'd just feel a prayer.

L.M. MONTGOMERY

Anne of Green Gables

Teach me

how to pray
and guide me
in what to pray about.

Help me

not to impose my own will
when I'm praying,
but rather enable me to pray
that your will be done.

Any concern too small to be turned into a prayer is too small to be made into a burden.

CORRIE TEN BOOM

IN ISAIAH 58, GOD TELLS of all the wonderful things that will happen when we fast and pray. He says, "You shall raise up the foundations of many generations; and you shall be called the Repairer of the Breach" (Isaiah 58:12). God wants us to restore unity, to maintain the family bonds in the Lord, and to leave a spiritual inheritance of solidarity that can last for generations.

Knowing that intercessory prayer is our mightiest weapon and supreme call for Christians today, I pleadingly urge our people everywhere to pray…Let there be prayer at sunup, at noonday, at sundown, at midnight, all through the day. Let us all pray for our children, our youth, our aged, our pastors, our homes. Let us pray for our churches.

ROBERT E. LEE

I know I need you to help me. I want to partner with you and partake of your gifts of wisdom, discernment, revelation, and guidance.

I also need your strength and patience, along with a generous portion of your love flowing through me.

teach me

how to love the way you love.
where i need to be healed, delivered,
changed, matured, or made whole,
i invite you to do that in me.

Help me

to walk in *righteousness*
and integrity before you.

WE BECOME THE PERSON God created us to be when we ask God for guidance and then do what He tells us to do.

Something amazing happens to our hearts when we pray for another person. The hardness melts. We become able to get beyond the hurts, and forgive. We even end up loving the person we are praying for. It's miraculous! It happens because when we pray we enter into the presence of God and He fills us with His Spirit of love…Prayer is the ultimate love language. It communicates in ways we can't.

Prayer gives rise to love, love begets more prayer, which in turn gives rise to more love. Even if your praying is not born out of completely selfless motives, your motives will become more unselfish as prayer continues.

Take my

selfishness, impatience, and irritability
and turn them into kindness, long-suffering,
and the willingness to bear all things.

Take my

old emotional habits, mindsets, automatic
reactions, rude assumptions, and self-protective
stance, and make me patient, kind, good,
faithful, gentle, and self-controlled.

take the

hardness of my heart
and break down
the walls with your battering
ram of revelation.

give me

a new heart and work in me
your love, peace, and joy. I am
not able to rise above who I am.
only you can transform me.

I'VE FOUND THAT PRAYER is the only thing that always works. The safeguard you have with prayer is that you have to go through God to do it. This means you can't get away with a bad attitude, wrong thinking, or incorrect motives. When you pray, God reveals anything in your personality that is resistant to His order of things.

God answers sharp
and sudden on some prayers,
And thrusts the thing
we have prayed for in our face.

ELIZABETH BARRETT BROWNING

And prayer is more
Than an order of words,
the conscious occupation
Of the praying mind,
or the sound of the voice praying.

T. S. ELIOT

Lord,

Your word says, "He who loves his brother abides in the light, and there is no cause for stumbling in him.

But he

who hates his brother is in darkness and walks in darkness, and does not know where he is going, because the darkness has blinded his eyes" (1 John 2: 10-11).

show me

places where i walk
in the darkness
of unforgiveness.

i don't

want that in my life.
i want to see clearly
and know where i'm going.

Do not be anxious about anything, but in everything, by prayer and petition, with thanksgiving, present your requests to God. And the peace of God, which transcends all understanding, will guard your hearts and your minds in Christ Jesus.

PHILIPPIANS 4:6-7

EVERYONE GOES THROUGH HARD times. It's nothing to be ashamed of. Sometimes our prayers help us to avoid them. Sometimes not. It's the attitude we have when we go through them that matters most. If we are filled with anger and bitterness, or insist on complaining and blaming God, things tend to turn out badly. If we go through them with thankfulness and praise to God, He promises to bring good things despite them. He says "count it all joy when you fall into various trials, knowing that the testing of your faith produces patience" (James 1:2-3).

Whether it feels like it or not, when we serve God, His love attends every moment of our lives—even the toughest, loneliest, most painful and desperate. He is always there in our midst, working things out for good when we pray and look to Him to do so.

Thank you, Lord,

that you suffered
and died for us
so that we might
be healed.

i lay claim

to that heritage of healing
which you have promised
in your word and provided
for those who believe.

i look to you

for a life of health,
healing, and wholeness.

freedom

ISN'T IT COMFORTING TO know that when we feel imprisoned by the death grip of our circumstances, God hears our cries for freedom? He sees our need…Who doesn't need that?

Now, brethren, if you sow seed you may be very feeble,
but it is not your hand that puts the seed into the ground
which produces the harvest—it is the vitality in the seed.
And so in the prayer of faith. When you can plead a
promise and drop that prayer into the ground with hope,
your weakness shall not make it miscarry; it shall still
prevail with God and bring down blessings from on high.

CHARLES SPURGEON

I confess

my own sins to you
and ask for forgiveness,
knowing your word says,

"If we confess

our sins, He is faithful and just to
forgive us our sins and cleanse us
from all unrighteousness"
(1 John 1:9).

praying

THE BOTTOM LINE IS, keep praying and don't give up. Sometimes prayers are answered quickly, but many are not. Jesus said, "Men always ought to pray and not lose heart" (Luke 18:1). Keep praying and you *will* see God answer. And don't worry about how the answers will be manifested. You don't have to make them happen. It's *your* job to pray. It's *God's* job to answer. Trust Him to do His job.

Prayer is
The world in tune,
A spirit-voice,
And vocal joys,
Whose echo is Heaven's bliss.
HENRY VAUGHN

Lord, you have said

in your word that if we
regard iniquity in our hearts,
you will not hear (psalm 66:18).

I want you to
hear my prayers,

so I ask you to reveal where there is
any disobedience in my life.

show me where

I have not obeyed you or lived your way.
I confess it as sin and ask for your forgiveness.

THE GOOD THING ABOUT prayer—or the problem with prayer, depending on your perspective—is that we have to go to God to do it. This means we can't get away with anything. It means that any negative thoughts, bad attitudes, hardness of heart, or selfish motives are going to be revealed by the Lord. Fervent and honest prayer causes the depths of our hearts to be exposed. That can be uncomfortable.

Let us pray for ourselves, that we may not lose the word "concern" out of our Christian vocabulary. Let us pray for our nation. Let us pray for those who have never known Jesus Christ and redeeming love, for moral forces everywhere, for our national leaders. Let prayer be our passion. Let prayer be our practice.

ROBERT E. LEE

hearts

OUR HEARTS HAVE TO be right when we pray. We all—men and women alike—jeopardize our own prayers when we don't pray them from a right heart. What is in our hearts when we pray has more effect on whether our prayers are answered than the actual prayer itself.

Thy servants, at this sacred hour,

With humble prayer thy throne surround,

That here, in glory and in power,

That light may shine, that voice may sound.

WILLIAM CULLEN BRYANT

*L*ord,
I know that you have
"called us to peace"
(1 corinthians 7:15).

Help us
to hear that call and live
in the peace that passes
all understanding.

IF WE ARE NOT POSITIONED right in our relationship to the Lord, we never catch the wind of His Spirit that enables us to sail against the tide of our limitations and circumstances and arrive at our destination. We keep coming back to the same old places, and we never get free. And the ride can get rough and unpleasant. We sometimes lose control and get the feeling that we're sinking. But when we move with the Spirit of God, He never leaves us to wander around where we are. He moves us on to where we are supposed to be. If we don't seek that fresh wind of God's Spirit to carry us, we never arrive at that place of wholeness and peace.

He who has learned how to pray
has learned the greatest secret
of a holy and a happy life.

WILLIAM LAW

Holy spirit,

i invite you to fill our home
with your peace, truth,
love, and unity.

Through

wisdom let our house be built,
and by understanding
may it be established.

by knowledge

may the rooms be filled with all precious
and pleasant riches (proverbs 24:3-4).

reveal to us

anything that is in our house
that is not glorifying to you, lord.
i say that "as for me and my house,
we will serve the lord" (joshua 24:15).

hope

THE MOST PROFITABLE WAY to invest in the future is to pray. God promises to give us a future and a good reason to have hope, but we have to pray about it (Jeremiah 29:11).

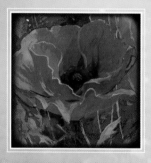

More holiness give me,
more striving within;
More patience in suffering,
more sorrow for sin;
More faith in my Saviour,
more sense of His care;
More joy in His service,
more purpose in prayer.

PHILIP BLISS
"My Prayer"

Help me

to be the kind of spiritual leader
that you want me to be.

increase

my faith, for i know that you
are a shield to those who put
their trust in you (proverbs 30:5).

you are

our refuge and our fortress. you are our god,
and in you will we trust (psalm 91:2).

We are Thine;
do Thou befriend us,
Be the guardian of our way;
Keep Thy flock from sin, defend us,
Seek us when we go astray.

Blessed Jesus, blessed Jesus
Hear, O hear us when we pray;
Blessed Jesus, blessed Jesus,
Hear, O hear us when we pray.

DOROTHY A. THRUPP